Golf Swing Tips

Simple Techniques to Drive the Ball for Distance and Accuracy

Larry Duncan

This book is dedicated to golf players who want to improve their swing and improve their game.

Copyright Act of 1976, the scanning, uploading and electronic sharing of any part of this book without the explicit written consent or permission of the publisher constitutes unlawful piracy and the theft of intellectual property.

If you would like to use material or content from this book (other than for review purposes), prior written permission must be obtained from the publisher.

You can contact the publishing company at admin@speedypublishing.com. Thank you for not infringing on the author's rights.

Speedy Publishing LLC (c) 2014
40 E. Main St., #1156
Newark, DE 19711
www.speedypublishing.co

Ordering Information:
Quantity sales; Special discounts are available on quantity purchases by corporations, associations, and others. For details, contact the "Special Sales Department" at the address above.

This is a reprint book.

Manufactured in the United States of America

Table of Contents

Publisher's Notes i

Chapter 1: Introduction to Driving the Ball 1

Chapter 2: The Right Golf Ball 3

Chapter 3: Which Iron Will Improve Your Swing? 7

Chapter 4: How Your Stance Affects Your Swing 15

Chapter 5: Perfecting Your Swing 20

Chapter 6: Power Driving and Distance 28

Chapter 7: Tips to Stop Slicing the Ball 34

Chapter 8: Conclusion 39

Meet the Author 41

More Books by Larry Duncan 42

Publisher's Notes

Disclaimer

This publication is intended to provide helpful and informative material. It is not intended to diagnose, treat, cure, or prevent any health problem or condition, nor is intended to replace the advice of a physician. No action should be taken solely on the contents of this book. Always consult your physician or qualified health-care professional on any matters regarding your health and before adopting any suggestions in this book or drawing inferences from it.

The author and publisher specifically disclaim all responsibility for any liability, loss or risk, personal or otherwise, which is incurred as a consequence, directly or indirectly, from the use or application of any contents of this book.

Any and all product names referenced within this book are the trademarks of their respective owners. None of these owners have sponsored, authorized, endorsed, or approved this book.

Always read all information provided by the manufacturers' product labels before using their products. The author and publisher are not responsible for claims made by manufacturers.

Print Edition 2014

Chapter 1: Introduction to Driving the Ball

As a golfer you know how bad it can be if you are hitting the ball too short for each drive. It can cost you the game and a really bad score. If you need to learn how to hit the ball a bit further at each hole you need to read this book.

The purpose of this book is to teach you how you can improve your shot to give you more than fifty yards every time you hit the golf ball. There are a lot of factors that must be considered when you play golf.

These factors include the type of ball you are using, the irons, your stance, swing, how to power drive, and of course, how to fix your slice. Just one of these factors being off can cause you to have less of a drive than desired.

This book should be used as a guide to help you understand how you should properly stand as you hold your club. You will learn how the club should be facing to achieve specific shots, how to hit over a tree, out of the sand, and down the fairway with complete power. You will also learn where to put the weight in your body throughout the entire swing.

You might be giving it all you've got in your shot and still cannot hit the ball as far as you would like. You might think you need to lift weights and build up the muscles in your arms.

The power in your shot isn't about how strong your arms are. It is about the right ingredients of stance, swing, the way you hold the club, and much more.

When you have just the right swing you will find you can drive the ball as far as you need to when you golf. You can get the additional distance you are looking for when you know how to make the key ingredients work for you in your golf game.

Those additional yards will mean less par and a better score. You will be amazed with the improvements on your game.

Chapter 2: The Right Golf Ball

You might have an amazing swing but it won't do anything for you if you aren't using the right golf ball. There is no reason to be wasting a perfect swing if you are not using the right ball.

When you are golfing with the right golf ball it can take a few strokes off of a round. There are many ways to tell which type of golf ball you need to use when you play the game. These also will make a big difference with the distance you get when you hit the ball.

There are three different types of golf balls. These three different golf balls are known as balata, two-piece, or a ball with the combination of both of the two. There are many things you need to consider when you are choosing which of these balls you will use.

The first thing you need to think about is what you are looking for. Do you want to have the ultimate spin control and have a low handicap? The balata is the ball for you. This is a softer ball which includes a soft cover. The soft cover allows for the ball to have a little bit more spin. Professional golfers use the Balata when they play, including Tiger Woods.

If you are looking for more distance in your swing and you have a higher handicap then you need more control on the distance and durability. This means you need a hard cover ball. A two-piece ball includes a hard cover which will not create as much backspin. This way, you will be able to hit the ball a longer distance than you did before.

When choosing a ball to use the weather may play into your decision also. You also want to look at the conditions of the golf course. If the course has been soaked in rain the ball that will produce the least amount of spin and will travel further will be your best choice; the two-piece.

If the golf course is rock hard and scorched from the sun then the softer ball will be the best choice. This is because the softer ball will land softly and spin rather than bounce.

The half and half ball has a little of both the soft and hard combined. You might try this ball if the conditions seem to be just right and you need a little bit of distance but you are working on the spin control also. Hitting with the different balls will give you a good idea of the difference they make when you play the game.

Another way to tell which ball you need to choose also depends on your swing. If you have a relatively slow golf swing then you should consider the two-piece ball. Distance is essential and with a slow swing you need a ball that will help you travel further. When you are on the greens the disadvantage will be that the ball will not spin very much as you work closer to the hole.

Some of the balls you might consider for the two-piece include the Nike Juice, Pinnacle Platinum Feel, and the Titleist DT Carry & Roll. You can find a three-piece ball that offers the same benefits as the two piece balls called the Top-Flite Gamer.

Golfers who have a swing which is tour like, will swing one-hundred and ten miles per hour and higher. These golfers have the ability to compress their drives and long irons. They usually benefit more from using the softer ball.

Some of these golfers use a three or even a four-piece ball which allows them to generate around the greens easily. This category of a ball can be found as the Bridgestone Tour B330 Series, Nike One series, Callaway Tour series, TaylorMade TP, Titleist Pro V1, and more.

Another consideration you will find with balls is the price. The more pieces and softer the ball is the higher the cost of the ball. These multiplayers can cost more than forty dollars while the two-piece balls can run around twenty dollars.

When choosing a golf ball you should consider a few things. You may lack distance in your play because you are using the wrong type of golf ball. The softer and more expensive golf balls are for the professionals who can swing the club over one-hundred miles per hour.

You might think the most expensive is always the best but if you are not one of the best they will not help you. The best ball for a slow swinger are the cheaper two-piece golf balls. They will help you add distance to every long shot.

CHAPTER 3: WHICH IRON WILL IMPROVE YOUR SWING?

There are many things that need to be considered when you choose a set of golf clubs. These things include how to choose the right set of golf clubs. You need to know the differences between the different types of clubs, the materials, and more.

Understanding these things can help you make a better decision which clubs are right for you. You also need to know how to use your irons which includes the different positions and more.

The first thing you need is a basic set of golf clubs. There is no reason to carry more than fourteen clubs in your bag at a time and it is actually against USGA regulation if you do. Your bag should include two or three woods, two fairway woods and a driver, eight irons, and additional wedges. If you want a putter these are usually sold separately.

The shaft of an iron can make all of the difference in how far you are capable of hitting the ball. There are two primary types of shafts which include the steel and graphite.

Steel shafts are strong, provide more durability, and they are cheaper clubs. A set of clubs with steel shafts will provide greater consistency from each shaft. You might even have more control on your shots.

The thing about steel shafts to remember is that they are best for golfers with a faster swing. If you want to generate a good distance with these types of shafts you should be a strong golfer who is looking for control in your game.

Graphite is lighter than steel and is actually made in different variations. These clubs are more expensive and they are not as durable as steel. Because of the lightweight the graphite shafts allow for a faster swing which results in a bit more power.

You might be sacrificing a bit of control when you swing the club because of the speed. Graphite clubs are also much better if you want to absorb the shock sent to your wrist from the club after impact. Gloves also help with this.

Another thing to look for is something called flex. This is the bend in a shaft, also known as the whip. The flex of the shaft must match the speed of a golf swing. A flexible shaft is perfect for a beginner golfer who has a slower and less powerful swing.

The average golfer has a swing around seventy-five to ninety miles per hour which requires a regular shaft. A stiff or firm shaft should be used for golfers who have a swing over ninety miles per hour. The stiffer the golf clubs are the more control the golfer has over the ball.

Today there is a shaft called the uniflex that is designed to fit any type of swing.

Buying a Driver or Fairway Wood

Choosing the right driver and fairway wood can be difficult if you don't know how big the club head size is supposed to be. Here are a few tips.

When you are choosing a wood there are three different club head sizes to choose from. The standard club head size measures approximately 150-155 cubic centimeters. This size has a smaller sweet spot but will give you better control.

The midsize size measures around 195 cubic centimeters and offers a few benefits. This will give you a medium sized sweet spot and the club is also much lighter than the oversized club head.

The oversized club head is the biggest you can choose from. The club head can be found at sizes up to 300+ cubic centimeters. This adds for a very large sweet spot with any of the head sizes. This is much more difficult for you to control and is heavier than the other two variations.

The club head comes in two materials. These materials can only make a difference with the way they feel and the way they look. These materials are stainless steel and titanium. They also differ in price significantly.

Stainless steel is much less expensive and heavier than titanium. The look of a stainless steel club is more traditional and feels that way too. The head is smaller because of the heavy weight.

The titanium is much lighter and allows for the club to have a larger club head. There is a larger sweet spot and the club proves to be much more forgiving than the traditional stainless steel models.

The loft of a club face head makes a big difference in the distance you might hit the ball. You need to know how to choose the loft of your club if you want to add more distance.

Loft is the measurement of the angle of the clubface head. The greater the loft measurement is the greater the angle will be on the face of the club head. This will allow for more control of the ball but less distance in your shot. The less loft on the club face the greater the distance. The more distance you have, the less control you will have over the ball.

Your swing will also make a difference with the type of loft you need with your clubs. If you have a slow swing you want the highest loft. This means you will look for clubs with a 10.5 to 12 degree loft.

If you are an average golfer with an average swing then you need to find a loft of 9.5 to 10.5.

The professionals have the fastest swings and they will have the lowest loft at around 8 to 9.5. If you are swinging over 90 mph you might want this loft too.

Buying the Right Fairway Woods

Fairway woods are an excellent solution to the alternative to drivers off the tee and for long hard hitting irons like the 2-, 3-, or 4-irons. There are three factors which make the fairway woods the preferred club.

Many golfers feel more comfortable while standing over a long fairway with a longer and lower profile wood rather than a long iron that is harder to hit.

It is easier to get the ball in the air out of the fairway if you have a lower center of gravity. This is also true if you are in the rough or in the sand.

You can take advantage of more distance without having to over swing when you have a larger club instead of a long iron. You can also have more control with the length.

Many people are replacing their long irons with fairway woods. If you want to try to use a wood rather than an iron for these benefits of distance and control you might want to consider these few things.

A 5-wood has the equivalence of a 2-iron, 7-wood for a 3- or 4-iron, and a 9-wood for a 5-iron.

Choosing the Right Irons

The irons are used for the golf shots that are shorter. These might range from two-hundred yards or even less than one-hundred.

The ability of the golfer to hit the distance and the loft of the club head will be the determining factors for choosing the right iron. There are two primary types of irons which include the cast irons and the forged irons.

The cast irons have a cavity back construction which is also called perimeter weighting. The weight of the head is mostly around the outside. The cast irons have a larger sweet spot because more weight is put around the edges of the club face. These irons are best for beginners who miss the ball and they are also more forgiving than the forged irons.

There really isn't a weight distribution that occurs with the forged irons on the back of the club head. The center of gravity occurs in the center of the club head. An advanced player can use a forged iron for better trajectory because of the weight beging higher in the face. This iron allows for more accuracy also when you have missed hits.

Irons have the same types of club heads as the woods and they are also made with titanium and stainless steel. The less advanced players should play with the stainless steel irons because of the provided durability and consistency.

Wedges

There are four different types of wedges. Wedges are used to get yourself out of a tough spot and sometimes it may require a bit of a distance. The different types of wedges include the pitching wedge, sand wedge, gap wedge, and the lob wedge.

The pitching wedge is used for longer wedge shots from one-hundred and twenty-five yards. The sand wedge is used for the sand.

The gap wedge is considered a compromise between the sand and the pitching wedge.

The lob wedge might be used over an obstacle like a tree where you need some height weight the ball in the air but not quite so much distance.

Which Iron to Use

When you are using an iron there are different considerations based on how you need to hit the ball. There are three irons you should understand which include the short iron, mid-iron, and the long iron.

When you use a short iron the ball will be in the middle of the stance and the club will be slightly behind it. The right ball position is smack dab in the middle of your stance.

The apex of your swing should be a couple balls forward. This means that you will hit the ball at a steep angle, producing a big divot. Your feet will be closer to the ball than they will be when you use a long iron.

The mid-sized iron is used slightly different. The ball will not be right in the middle of your stance but it will be slightly forward. The longer the iron is the more forward the ball will need to be. You will still hit the ball with a hard blow but not as steep as you need with the short iron. The divot will also not be as deep either.

When you use a long iron the ball will be furthest from you. You want to hit the ball in a sweeping motion rather than hitting down on the ball. The best way to hit the ball is right at the apex of your swing arc.

There is no need to force the ball up by hitting the ball on the upswing. The ball will automatically become airborne because of the angle of the attack of the way you hit the ball.

Chapter 4: How Your Stance Affects Your Swing

The way you stand can make a big difference on the way you hit the ball. It can also dictate the distance of your shot. Your Swing means everything. The way you have your feet, you hold the club, where you are looking, and even how you shift your body weight all come into play when you hit the ball.

Your stance is very important when you intend to hit the ball. There are three different stances you should know which include square, open, and closed. One thing to consider is that it is usually best to use the same stance as the same clubface alignment.

For example, if you are using an open stance then you should use an open clubface. Never move the clubface angle in a position that contradicts the way you are standing.

When you use a stance that is square to the ball's target line you will influence the club to swing down the line a little bit longer than when you would if your stance is open or closed.

If you were to measure where most golfers were actually aiming you would see the square stance is most commonly used. An open or closed stance will actually influence the shoulders to follow through properly.

An open stance should be used when you are moving the ball from left to right. When you use an open stance you will align your stance slightly open. Your shoulders will swing the club across the ball. The wider your legs are the more open your stance is. The more open, the wider your shoulders will be also.

An open stance is a good solution for someone who tends to over swing on the ball. The curvature and the trajectory of your shot also depend on the amount you rotate the clubface when you address the ball. When you open the clubface you get a high trajectory but a shorter shot.

A closed stance is the best way to stand when you are moving the ball from right to left. That means your stance is slightly closed to the target line of the ball.

When your stance is closed your shoulders swing the club from the inside of your body. A closed stance is the best solution when you are trying to pick up distance on your swing. These shots will have less height but travel further.

The Best Posture

There are a few things you need to do in order to have good posture when you are preparing to hit the ball. You need to think about standing tall, bending, and your posture.

If you want to hit the ball well and get the distance you need to stand properly with perfect posture. If you do not have the perfect posture there will have to be some type of compensation in your swing if you want to deliver the ball on the right path.

You must have a perfectly flat back while you are standing. Flatten your back up against your iron and be sure it is flat. This will help with your posture.

When you hold the club and as you move you need to bend from your hips. Bend from the hips as you bring the club to the back and head. If you are someone who rounds their shoulders or maintains straight legs the club will not be able to remain in place.

You have to flex your knees in an athletic looking position. Flex your knees into a position as if you were playing baseball waiting for someone to hit the ball to you in the field.

Now you have a flat back and your legs are flexed. The angle between your chest and your club should be at a 90 degree angle. Your belt and your club shaft should also be on the same plane. You can check your posture in a mirror if you are not sure if you have the right stance.

The Grip of Your Golf Club

There are three different types of grips when you hold a golf club. Not everyone uses the same grip. When you are using the proper grip on your golf club it will feel natural and very comfortable to you.

There are certain fundamentals that you should use in order to have the right golf grip. The different types of golf grips include the overlap, interlocking and the ten finger.

The overlap grip is the most common grip for most players. This grip became popular around the turn of the 20th century. This is also the most common grip taught by instructors for beginners also. The club is actually held in the fingers.

To use the overlap grip you will place your lay out your hand and lay the club in your fingers with your pinkie finger opened. The thumb will fit on the lead hand that is gripped around the club. The lead hand's thumb will fit in the lifeline of the trailing hand. If you are a right handed golfer, your lead hand will be your left hand.

The interlocking grip is the next most common grip. This grip is popular with the professional golfers. This grip interlocks the hands together. There is risk involved with this grip because the stray could lead into the palms of the hands. This style of grip is preferred by most people who have weak forearms and wrists, small hands, and for beginners.

When you want to use the interlocking grip you will take the little finger on the trailing hand (if you are right handed, the trailing hand is your right hand) and intertwine it with the index finger of the left hand or the lead hand. The thumb of the lead hand will fit into the lifeline of the trailing or right hand.

The ten finger grip is also known as the baseball grip because you will hold the club as you would a baseball bat. This is most preferred among the golf instructors.

There are advantages to this type of grip. Instructors prefer this grip because it makes instruction easy. When learning the interlocking grip it can be confusing and cause problems. This is a basic grip and easy to do. Someone who experiences joint pain, arthritis, weak hands, and other problems may prefer this type of grip.

When you use the ten finger grip you will position your hands properly starting with the lead hand grip. Place your little finger against the index finger of the trailing hand. Both hands will grip the club tightly and be pushed up against one another.

CHAPTER 5: PERFECTING YOUR SWING

There are many ingredients to a good swing. You can have great shoes, clubs, balls and these things will not matter if you have a bad swing. If you want to add distance to your shot you need to focus on your swing with each and every shot.

Many golfers spend years trying to perfect their swing. This can be a life-long challenging objective. Focusing on a few simple things can help you minimize any chances of missing the ball, slicing the ball, and not getting the distance you are trying to achieve. This will result in fewer strokes it will take you to get the ball to the hole on every run.

The most important thing is your posture. Be sure you have excellent posture before you hit the ball. Align the club directly in front of you as you stand with your back perfectly straight. Your left arm should also be extended and straight. You should be comfortable in this stance.

It is important to remember this swing is designed for a right handed golfer. When a right handed golfer is in this stance and practicing this swing a left handed golfer can stand directly in front of this person and look as if you are standing in the mirror to achieve the exact same results.

You will lift your left shoulder while you are lowering your right shoulder. You will not put your weight on the right foot or lean to the right either. Be sure your stance remains straight upward as you lift and lower your shoulders vertically. While you are lowering the right shoulder, your right arm will be touching the lower right side of your stomach.

With this form you will be sure you are in the proper starting posture. This will also be almost the same posture when the club makes contact with the ball. Thinking about this stance helps you reduce any possibility of missing the ball or resulting in a poor strike.

The plane is the area that surrounds the body, chest and stomach. This is your next focus. You need to see three points; the handle, the spot where your arm is touching your stomach, and the far side of your right hip. These three points are the swing plane.

As you swing the club you will pull it back bending your right elbow slightly maintaining a straight left arm. The clubface will actually come up over your head. When you come down in your downswing this is where the force and the speed of the swing come into play and it is a very important factor of your swing.

Be sure you come down with force on the shot as you extend your right arm. Your weight will actually shift to your right leg. As you make contact with the ball you will follow through with the club.

Your left arm should be used to guide the swing also. Your torso will turn toward the fairway as you would be watching the ball in flight. In the follow through your right arm will be straight and your left arm will now be bent.

Practicing your swing is very important. There are many reasons your swing could be the cause of not enough distance. You don't have to be hitting a ball to practice your swing.

However, you can spend hours at a driving range to practice your swing with the different types of clubs so you can get a good idea of the distance you can hit the ball with the different sizes of clubs.

Practice is everything when it comes to your swing. If you don't know how to properly swing the club then you may never get it right.

Your hands should remain low in the follow through of your swing. The higher your hands are the more trajectory you will have in the ball. The importance is distance. You want the ball flight to remain low.

It is also important to be sure you are on the plane at the top of your swing. If you want to guarantee accuracy and a solid strike you must be on plane as you reach the club face at the top of your swing (above your head). Your right forearm should be parallel to your spine.

Your left wrist should be flat and your elbows and arms will form a tight triangle. When these factors are true you will also ensure you rotate your shoulders properly in the backswing.

Your body provides the power when you use it properly. You do not get your power from your arms. In order to use your body properly you will put the club behind the ball at address. Your body will be in a dead stop position.

You cannot move the ball in this position comfortably. When you use the club with your body you will find that you can get the ball in the air more consistently. On your downswing you will also turn fully.

You also need to gain control over the length of your swing if you want a solid contact with the ball. The left arm and the club shaft should have a forty-five degree angle upon setup. This will start the swing with the wrists hinged halfway to the ninety degree angle you need to be at.

In the takeaway the hands will remain close to the ground while the club head moves upward quickly. The goal is to have the left thumb pointed down at the right shoulder as quickly as you can.

The way you can tell if you achieve this properly is by looking at your left arm. It should be parallel to the ground and the club shaft should be perpendicular to it also. You will hinge your wrists in the backswing and this will result in a consistent distance and direction on all of your iron shots no matter the distance.

Part of your swing needs to focus on the right elbow and the shoulder tilt. You need to be sure you do not have a faulty shoulder that causes you to slice the ball. The best position for the right elbow is inside the seam running down the right side of your shirt.

When your elbow remains in the seam of your shirt this will allow for the shoulders to turn level to your spine. This will make it easy to drop the club inside on the downswing which will result in maximum power and as much control as possible.

If you have a solid plane you will not slice the ball. This is a factor that can help avoid the slice anyway. At the point of contact you want to be sure you do not have an open face. The swing path often tends to come too much on the outside which can cause problems with your contact and direction also. Every golfer's swing path must come from the inside.

When you are in your backswing it is important to remember not to stiffen your leg. If you do stiffen your back leg you will tilt out of balance. This will make it difficult to rebend your knee upon impact of the ball.

Many golfers refer to the angle you form in your back leg by the upper and lower leg the special K. The angle should be maintained from the moment of address to after the impact in order to maintain a level swing. The best way to practice the special K is to swing in the mirror and watch your position.

When you are in the setup of the special K your body will look like you are in a position that is ready for action. At the address you will flex your back knee while you swing. All your body has to do is rotate if you are prepared correctly. Your lower leg needs to be straight up and down. This special K position unlocks your hips so they can rotate properly.

Upon impact the arm that trails needs to snap straight to release the power into the ball. The back kneed will kick toward the target while remaining in the special K flex. After impact both of your arms will be straight and the club head will be below the hands. The butt of the club should be pointed toward the middle of the body.

You will also maintain the special K position in your backswing. This will allow your elbows to remain level near the top of the swing. This will result in keeping the clubface from twisting out of the position you need it to be in.

Using the special K position of the backswing will help the club shaft travel along the right swing path as you gradually gain power while the club ascends to the target.

Typical Problems with a Swing

There are many factors in a swing that can cause you to lose distance with your shot. These things can be easy to fix if you can identify what you are doing wrong with your swing. Here are many different things you might do with your swing that can be repaired.

A reverse pivot occurs when you turn your body too far and you do not shift the weight from your left front foot. This will force you to lunge behind the ball and actually scoop it. This is known as a fat shot. You might even pop the ball up on accident when you do this.

If you want to avoid a reverse pivot you will need to manage your weight properly when you swing the club. The most of your body mass needs to shift to your back foot during your backswing.

You must remember that shifting and sliding isn't the same thing. A proper weight shift occurs when you turn. The body will turn away and the weight will naturally move to the back foot.

Turning is a big factor when it comes to power. As you turn and move shift the weight you are loading your back leg with torque. This puts you in the best position to come down hard and fast on the downswing for the unwind. When you turn properly you will unwind faster and hit the ball harder.

You can also lose distance in your shot when you have a late wrist cock. This can also result in swaying. This component of a swing is the most overlooked but is very common. An amateur golfer may think the less wrist cock the better accuracy but this is not the case.

When you cock your wrist properly it can actually help you rotate your body more effectively. This will also increase the speed to the ball. You must set your wrist earlier. Once your hands reach your waist in the swing they should be in the 90 degree angle. Your left arm will be straight while your right elbow still tucked into your side.

This will provide for an efficient rotation while you swing. The wrist cock also helps you prevent dipping your shoulder also. The proper wrist cock allows you to swing with a level shoulder plane.

When you release too early you can also lose power in your shot. Releasing your hands too early is a myth many amateur golfers thing is the right thing to do. You are at risk of losing your club too. The cause of this may be from an overactive right hand.

The best way to avoid a problem of releasing the club too quickly is to turn your body prior to releasing the hands.

Chapter 6: Power Driving and Distance

Driving is one of the most important aspects you need to conquer when golfing. You need to be able to have a power drive to hit the ball straight and with distance.

Many people have a hard time hitting the ball a long distance and find this is where they find they add extra strokes onto their play. If you could just hit the golf ball a little further then you would have a better game. There are many ways you can focus on your drive to make your game more successful and enjoyable.

Managing your drive is very important. You need to focus on your strengths right off of the tee. This will help you be a better player. If you know how you normally hit the ball you can try changing your drive to make use of it.

For example, if you find that you most often hit the ball and the ball flight usually curves to the left then you might want to stand near the right side of the tee. This can help make up for a left curve.

There are two things that must be considered when you want to hit the ball long. These things include making solid contact with the golf ball and an increased club head speed.

If you can obtain the ability to swing the club consistently on the same swing plane while maintaining control of the clubface you will be able to make solid contact. Snapping your hips through the ball as you make contact will also help with increasing the speed.

The best way to hit with an ascending blow is to tee the ball well forward in your stance. Never allow roll. Your wrist should not break down in the takeaway and your arms need to be fully extended. This will create a wide arc for your club to travel.

Your shoulders should be turning around your body. Never place too much weight at the front of your body. Be sure to shift your weight properly as you swing.

The wrong hip rotation can cause you to lose power in your swing. Most golfers slide their hips laterally rather than rotate them counterclockwise.

When doing a lateral slide it will create a problem that can cause a slice or a hook which will result in a lack of power. You can also hurt your back.

Proper movement of the hips is essential to the power of your stroke. When the hips are more open than the shoulders as the club is delivered into the ball is the best way to store power and deliver it directly into the impact.

In addition, when the hips are cleared it will help maintain the proper spine angle through impact. This will promote the right weight shift for solid contact.

A good drive requires power and total control. When trying to achieve power and control you need to properly release the club through impact. You also need a strong left to right ball flight. The proper way to do this is to move your arms and club left following impact.

If you are trying to achieve a shot that is lower moving left to right you want to move your hands to the left immediately after impact. Keep the shaft angled. Your forearms will not rotate upon impact and the clubface will remain slightly opened.

If you want to achieve a right to left ball flight you want to allow the club head to pas your hands following impact of the golf ball. This will allow for an inside attack. You want to achieve transferring more energy to the ball than you normally do which will help you get a higher right to left stroke.

Setup is essential to giving your drive more power. You must setup your swing properly. You should use a wood or a driving iron to properly setup for your drive because of the length of the clubs. Using a longer club will give you two advantages.

You will be able to increase the distance of your stance away from the ball and this will also allow you to spread your feet wider. This will allow you to balance your weight as you transfer it in your swing. This way you can get a short but wider swing which will allow for total control and power which will all have the proper proportions.

The sequence of motion is very important to understand in your setup and your swing. The sequence should be in order from setting up, swinging, and driving as you use the proper weight transfer.

This is very hard for amateur golfers but it is important to maintain the sequence. Developing your game on this sequence can help with a more powerful stroke.

Your power needs to build up entirely and then be released entirely upon impact. Building power begins in the swing. Always release your power when you make impact with the ball. The swing needs to remain short.

You will have less control over your stroke the longer your swing is. Many beginners think that if you have to swing long to hit far. A short and wide swing will provide the most power and control over your stroke.

Maintaining balance is very important. To accomplish this you must swing within yourself. As you swing be sure you do not swing too far back or forward. Be sure to remain within yourself so you are in control. This will help you evenly distribute your weight from heel to toe.

You must be sure to maintain good posture, keep your spine aligned straight and your chin should be upright. These things will help you avoid injury and knock the ball down the fairway with power.

Remember when you drive the ball you don't ever need to swing as hard as you can as if you are playing baseball. You might have the same type of swing but be swinging in a different swing plane. However you do not need big muscles to make the golf ball go a long distance.

Many very good golfers are very thin and they have the ability to hit at very long distances. It is all about leverage. Once you master the leverage in your swing you will be able to add the distance to your shots also.

Focus on the angle you create between the club and your left hand. This angle needs to be held as long as you can. If you force yourself to hold this angle it may result in a poor swing. Some golfers like to think of the club as a whip.

One of the best ways to create the leverage is to begin the downswing with a shift of your hips in the direction of the target.

This will help build the power you are storing so you can release it in the impact of the ball.

You also need to be sure to swing within your limits and nothing more. When you swing as hard as you can it is silly. Focus on your swing and be sure to swing as free as you can with control.

If you find that it is common for you to lose balance in your swing then you are most likely swinging too hard.

When you swing the golf club comfortably rather than stretching or swinging too hard you will be able to achieve more distance by launching the ball with the right spin and trajectory. This is the best way for you to hit the ball as far as you can and straight.

Your focus should be on accuracy and after time your distance will improve also.

When you are on the golf course you cannot be out there practicing. Meaning, don't focus on the mechanics. You should have practiced the mechanics enough to be able to trust your swing now.

If you can trust your swing you will be able to swing better and hit the ball with a more solid strike. Launching the ball with good spin and trajectory happens when you trust your swing.

Chapter 7: Tips to Stop Slicing the Ball

A golf slice can be devastating and very frustrating to a golfer. There are many factors that could cause you to slice the ball. If you find you slice the ball quite often then you will need to fix it.

If you want to improve your overall game and add distance to your shots. Imagine how far the ball would go if you could just straighten out your shot.

A golf slice occurs when your club is open upon impact of the club and relative to the path of the club head.

A wayward left hand is one of the common factors that can cause you to slice the ball far to the right. This happens more often than you would think. When a wayward left hand occurs the back of your left hand will be aligned to the right of the ball and the clubface will be open. This will cause a slice to happen.

If you want to repair a wayward left hand it is important to focus on the back of your hand. The back of your hand should be facing the target at impact. You should at least feel that the back of your hand is facing your target. This will allow you to have a strong grip for the shot so your hand doesn't slip.

It is important to square your left hand. One of the best ways to do this is by practicing without using a club at all. You will stand with your right arm to the side of your body and rotate your left forearm. Then you will cock your left wrist and swing back. In order to be sure your hand is square practice your swing repeatedly without your club in your hand.

A weak grip is a common factor and cause of a wayward left hand causing the ball to slice far in one direction, usually the right. A weak grip will cause you to turn your hands too far to the left in your swing. You might have a square back hand and find that you are still slicing the ball. This is common for golfers who have a very weak grip.

You must tighten your grip on the club when you swing with all of your might on a long driver. You can fix this also by turning your hands to the right on the club while you are maintaining a good position with the club in your hands.

One of the things to remember is that when you focus on maintaining a strong grip you will also have a hard time with the way you turn the club. This is because it is very easy to turn your left hand over. This will make it easier so you don't have to go far for the club to be square. But it is the wrong position.

You must keep one thing in mind while you are attempting to maintain the right grip and square. If you are attempting to square your left hand and you find that you are unable to it will mean something else.

Although you are trying to fix your slice you are looking in the wrong place. Not being able to correct the slice by squaring your wrists can mean that you have something wrong with your swing instead of the grip.

Another thing that can cause you to slice the ball is when you have far too much of a steep plane in your swing. This can definitely cause the ball to go in the direction you didn't mean to.

Swinging the ball too steep makes it far too difficult for your hands to have the ability to turn over. This also means you will be unable to turn over and square your club with the impact of the ball.

If you have a very steep plane in your swing and the tendency to slice the ball because of this then you can fix it. This type of swing is a natural consequence from things that force you to hit downward. Don't hit the ball downward. That is what causes the slice.

If you are a golfer that swings the club straight up and then straight down it will cause you to block the open face. This is because you will reverse rotate through the impact. The importance is to swing the club around the body as if you are swinging a baseball club.

You might even pretend you are swinging a baseball club outward. Now, take your club and pretend your baseball is down on the ground. You are only changing the swing plane when you swing the club versus the baseball bat. Many instructors will teach you this and you can try it. This is a good technique for amateur golfers to try because it really helps.

The shoulder tilt is another thing that can cause you to slice the ball. If you have an embarrassing slice then you need to look at the way you are moving your shoulders. The problem is not stemming from your arms moving up and down. This is a common mistake people think when they try to correct it.

When a shoulder tilt occurs the body is not tilting and not turning as it is supposed to be. Your arms have nothing to do with it. In order to correct a shoulder tilt you want to swing your arms around your body.

One way to get the swing right is to cross your arms around your chest and turn back and forth in a pivot. Once you have your shoulder swing down then you can place a club in your hands and practice swinging the club properly.

Some golfers have a really good golf swing. They look at all of the factors and cannot figure out what is causing the problem. The final thing you want to look at is if you are rotating the clubface too much when it is moved away from the ball. This happens often and it causes you to open the face of the club too far and then you have a further distance to square the ball again upon impact.

It is important to be sure the club is square in your back swing. Instead of rotating the club open verify the club is square. If you are unsure where in your swing to verify this, check your club when your swing is at two o'clock. The club should be square when you are holding the club in this position.

A problem slicing the ball can stem from many different factors. Every step of a swing could have a problem that could cause you to slice to ball. The way to determine what it is causing your slice is to check out your entire swing from the way you are gripping the club, opening the clubface, shifting your weight, and more. You might even find something wrong that will help you even more.

Repairing a slice in the golf game can make a big difference to the score at the end of your round. Not only will you gain serious distance with the shot but you will have hit a straight ball. This means you won't need to hit the ball again just to recover it out of the sand or rough either.

CHAPTER 8: CONCLUSION

Adding power to your game and distance to your shots doesn't mean you need to do a little body building and arm strengthening. There are many factors that can take away distance when you golf. When you understand these things you can add greater distances to your shots every single game.

The club you use depends greatly on how well you swing the club. This also depends on your swing speed and more. You must consider the shafts, materials and more when you choose a set of clubs.

You cannot use your friend's clubs and expect to have a good game. A good set of clubs should be measured and determined by your swing and your comfort factor.

The type of ball you use to golf will be determined by the way you swing the clubs also. You need to determine the weather and course conditions too. These things will also make a difference with the type of ball you choose and getting the most distance from your shot.

Many of the other factors you need to consider in order to add more distance to your shot every single time you play golf include your stance, your weight shift, your swing, wrists, shoulders, and more.

There are many factors to your swing and if you are lacking distance you need to look at the way you are building up and transferring the power to the ball on impact.

Correcting errors in the way you play can help you add distance to your game. You might be using the wrong type of ball or club, or just need to straighten out your slice. You can do these things when you know which factors to look for.

Now you can get out on the course and play golf like a pro because you know how to add the distance to your play.

Meet the Author

Larry Duncan grew up in Pasadena California and his love for the game of golf stems from his father. With hand me down clubs from his older brothers, Larry hit the golf course with his dad at the age of five. Larry's brothers became more interested in girls and cars rather than golfing with dad but Larry took advantage of this one-on-one time alone with his father.

Larry practiced, played every chance and fell in love with golf's challenges and sportsmanship. Larry played in Junior Leagues and tournaments and also played all four years on his high school golf team.

Larry continued to play recreationally in college while focusing on his education. Larry has enjoyed a career as a physical education teacher at a community college and teaches strength training and golf. When not teaching golf to students Larry loves to play and schedules weekend trips and vacations to courses on his bucket list.

More Books by Larry Duncan

Golf Basics 101: A Beginner's Guide to Equipment, Terminology and Understanding Your Clubs

Golf: How to Improve Your Game: The Ultimate Golf Guide for Beginners

www.ingramcontent.com/pod-product-compliance
Ingram Content Group UK Ltd.
Pitfield, Milton Keynes, MK11 3LW, UK
UKHW050415240426
12048UKWH00020B/1521